T0159140

The Scuba Snobs' Guide to Diving Etiquette

Debbie and Dennis Jacobson

authorHOUSE®

AuthorHouse™
1663 Liberty Drive
Bloomington, IN 47403
www.authorhouse.com
Phone: 1-800-839-8640

First published by AuthorHouse 5/31/2011

ISBN: 978-1-4634-0347-8 (sc)
ISBN: 978-1-4634-0346-1 (e)

Library of Congress Control Number: 2011908248

Printed in the United States of America

Scuba Snobs is a Registered trademark of Dennis J. Jacobson

Contents

Chapter 1

How We Became Known As The Scuba Snobs

Debbie has been a certified diver since 2002, and has over 150 ocean dives. Dennis was certified in 1998, earned his professional dive master credential in 2000, and has over 500 dives, of which two thirds are ocean dives. We both love diving, and we love meeting divers. We are active divers, averaging at least two dive destination trips per year. Dennis gets another thirty to forty dives per year while training and instructing in local reservoirs. We both make it a point to mark a little pool time before dive trips if we have been out of the water more than ninety days.

Our daughter does not dive (yet) but has heard us talk of dive trips and been with us on some. A few years ago after hearing one of the stories in this book she looked at us and said, "You guys are really Scuba Snobs." She was right. We are not only avid divers who love everything about diving, but we have worked hard to acquire and maintain those skills that competent divers exhibit. What makes us Scuba Snobs is not that we have those skills and habits as active divers. What makes us Scuba Snobs is that *we expect other divers to have them too.* When we find ourselves diving with those who don't, we have a tendency to talk about them, and not in a good way.

New divers are usually a delight on a dive. They have retained the skills they were taught, they are likely to practice what they were taught, and they seldom overestimate their own skills (though it happens). Active divers, who themselves may qualify as Scuba Snobs are also appropriate on dives (usually). Unfortunately there are a whole lot of divers out there who have either (a) never learned good diving habits, or (b) forgotten them somewhere along the line, or (c) are just plain jerks. As a favor to them, but mostly to the divers who do know how to behave above and below the water, we offer this handy guide.

We hope you will have a good laugh and be amused, but we also hope you (or the person you've really bought this book for) will be a better diver and dive companion for having read it. Good manners are always appropriate, regardless of a diver's skill level.

This book is for recreational divers. It presents *our* rules of etiquette for recreational diving. It is not about commercial diving or technical diving. Being a commercial diver or technical diver doesn't qualify you to be a Scuba Snob. You might qualify, but not because of some certificate or license. Scuba Snobs can be those with only a basic open water certification, or they can be divers with professional ratings. It's not about credentials. It's about skills, good diving habits. and good manners and common courtesy in and out of the water.

Chapter 2

Qualifications To Be A Scuba Snob

To be a Scuba Snob you must be an avid and *active diver.* You must have *excellent scuba skills.* That means you have excellent buoyancy control, stay close to your buddy, and do safe and proper ascents. Yet more is required to earn the title Scuba Snob and all it represents. Having skills is important, but you must *exercise those skills.* You also must *own your own scuba gear.* That gear needs to be of good quality, properly maintained, and you need to know how to use it. Snobs do not, however, over-equip themselves. Being a "techie" doesn't qualify you to be a Scuba Snob. Nor does having any particular rating or level of certification. Having a dozen specialty certifications, a master scuba diver rating, advanced or rescue diver rating mean nothing if you do not possess *and practice* the skills of a competent and safe **and sociable** diver. Also, unless you are diving in kelp forests or acting in a movie, if you have a dive knife with a blade six inches or longer strapped to your calf, you cannot be a Scuba Snob.

Scuba Snobs have done some diving. It's really hard to qualify as a Scuba Snob unless you have a *minimum of fifty, and in most cases, at least one hundred ocean dives*. It's not impossible, but it's very unlikely. It takes time to develop optimal skills and habits. Scuba Snobs *log all of their dives*, and *learn from every dive*. Scuba Snobs do not all look like world class athletes, but they are *in decent physical condition* and take care of themselves.

Scuba Snobs are *not air suckers*. Their skills, planning, proper weighting, proper equipment and proper securing of that equipment on their person, combined with decent health all lead to them being the ones who come back from every dive with a comfortable cushion of unused air in their tank (almost all of the time).

Scuba Snobs *listen to dive master briefings*. Scuba Snobs are *aware of and follow rules of the dive boat and rules and laws of the area where they are diving*. Scuba Snobs aren't pushy- they don't have to be. They are secure in the knowledge that they know what they are doing. Scuba Snobs occupy their space on the dive boat, set up their gear without elbowing others, and have *good manners above and below the water*.

Scuba Snobs are the people on the boat that other people want to be their dive buddy. They are fun to dive with and to be around. Everyone should work to qualify as a Scuba Snob.

Chapter 3

Rules Of Etiquette On The Day Boat

Most diving is done from boats that leave from the dock and return on the same day. These are day boats (or night boats, if taken for a night dive). Some are very small and offer no amenities. Others are large, equipped for 24 divers or more with multiple tanks for each diver. These boats often offer beverages, snacks, and sometimes even a real lunch. They usually have a head (toilet). To be a proper diver on a day boat, you must follow these rules of etiquette:

USE A BOAT BAG

This is the primary rule of etiquette for day boat diving. It cannot be over emphasized. For those who don't know, a boat bag is a soft mesh duffle bag that can be collapsed to the size of a shoebox or smaller. It will hold all your gear, and it will not be in the way on the boat. Get one. Use one.

We were once on a day boat out of Lahaina, Maui and a new diver had a huge hard case for his equipment that was the size of a steamer trunk. It was full of his gear and he plopped it right in the middle of the dive deck and left it there. Asshole! It was a real hazard for anyone trying to move around the boat, and he was in everyone's way as well. Get a boat bag, and you might one day be welcomed back on a dive boat. Not surprisingly, this person had other issues too, discussed in later chapters. Your oversized hard case does not belong on the day boat and neither does that gear bag you packed all your gear in to put on the airplane, bus, train or car that got you to your destination. These bags are big, heavy, and THEY DON'T BELONG ON A BOAT. Yet we see them constantly. Get a clue. Get a boat bag. There are thousands of scuba retailers who will be very happy to sell you one.

The flip side of this point is that having no bag at all is only slightly better than having the big inappropriate gear bag or suitcase or chest. The diver who has his/her hands full of gear, lunch, and other stuff and drops things all the way down the dock, or (worse still) on the boat and on our feet, is also being inconsiderate and is not our friend. Get a boat bag. They are cheap.

LISTEN TO THE BRIEFING

It doesn't matter if you dove the site yesterday, or dozens of times, or that you know the divemaster's name. On every dive, please shut up and listen to the divemaster's (and if applicable, the captain's) briefing. Conditions change, not everyone on the dive was along yesterday, and we need to hear the briefing. So do you. We do not need to hear your summary of yesterday's dive. The divemaster does not need your help. Give your monologue a rest for a few minutes already. This is an important rule. It is so important, in fact, that if a bona fide Scuba Snob ever violates it, they lose their status as a Scuba Snob for a while, maybe forever.

To listen to the briefing means you are not doing anything else during the briefing. You are not talking to other people, you are not taking a picture, and you are not still screwing around trying to figure out how to set up your gear. You are not fiddling with your camera or video. Do those things when everyone else is doing them. If you need help with your gear, ask the boat crew or dive leader, or, if you ask politely, you can ask someone else who seems to know what they are doing: a Scuba Snob. We can actually be helpful, even nice, and usually are.

KEEP YOUR STUFF OUT OF THE CAMERA BUCKET/WASH

Most but not all day boats will have a large bucket or barrel filled with fresh water into which cameras *and nothing else* are placed. These camera buckets give expensive photo and video equipment a safe ride and keep them out of everyone's way while on board. The camera bucket is not for you to dip your mask in, or to wash off your regulator or your computer or buoyancy vest or anything else. If you listened to the briefing you would know that.

Dennis once had a person actually dip his buoyancy vest and regulator in a camera bucket that contained several expensive pieces of camera and video gear (including his). Strobes were jostled, buttons pushed, general mayhem ensued, and yet the Scuba Snobs on board let the offender live. You may not be so lucky. Keep your crap out of the camera bucket.

DON'T SMOKE

Here is a simple rule: No smoking. No smoking of anything, at all. Don't even bring smoking materials on board, or a Scuba Snob on board will see that they hit the wet part of the deck. On a recent dive outing at an unnamed dive destination in Mexico, we had "the torch" puffing away all the way out to the dive sight. He was also the guy who of course geared up late, delayed the entry for everyone, and was the first guy out of air. Somehow (no one ever did take full responsibility) his pack of cigarettes hit the bottom of the boat and was soaked. He spent the entire boat ride back to shore trying to light a totally waterlogged cigarette. It was unbelievable. He looked totally ridiculous.

No one wants your smoke destroying the wonderful aroma of the salt air, and if you flick your butt into the ocean, you should be banned from all dive boats forever. Liveaboards (see Chapter 4) may have a place for you to engage in your habits, but day boats don't. And why is anyone even smoking at all these days? If you have a one-pack-a-day habit, over the course of a year you are spending the equivalent of the cost of an entire set of scuba gear, including a decent computer, just on your cigarettes. It also adds up to be the equivalent of the price of a dive trip with airfare to many fine Caribbean dive destinations. Do the math. It's your call. Smoking, or Grand Cayman for a week?

PUKE ONLY WHERE APPROPRIATE

Never puke on another diver. Never puke on the boat. Don't puke in the camera bucket either. Puke over the side of the boat. That's about all there is to it. Fish love puke, other divers do not. Also, try not to be too obvious when you puke. Dennis quite often pukes at the end of a dive. But he can be so subtle that on occasion even Debbie, who is sitting and gearing up right next to him, has to ask if he in fact puked. It's a gift.

PEE ONLY WHERE AND WHEN APPROPRIATE

The jury is in. The debate is over. It is ok to pee in your wetsuit when in the ocean. It is okay to climb back on the boat if you wait at least five minutes after peeing in your wetsuit in the ocean before re-boarding. It is not ok to pee in your wetsuit when on the boat. If you are on the boat and have to pee, and there is no head (toilet) on the boat, either hold it or jump in the water and pee. This works best if the boat is not moving and if you tell at least one other person, preferably a crew member, that you are jumping in for a minute. Once you have finished, wait five minutes and then re-board. Guys, it is **not ok** to lean over the gunwale, pull it out, and let fly. Ever. This is not ok for the ladies either, just in case you were wondering.

DON'T KICK, JOSTLE OR HIT OTHER DIVERS

This is a rule you might think doesn't need to be included here, but remember some day boats are quite small. On them entry into the water is usually done by everyone counting three and rolling backward at the same time. The point is to do this simultaneously but **without kicking the diver next to you.** One of our favorite places to dive has only these one-dive-at-a-time boats, and recently each of us received a knee/ fin/ something else to the face while rolling off these small boats. It was not good. On one dive Dennis had to descend maskless (with Debbie's help) to retrieve his mask 45 feet down because he got kicked in the face. Not cool, but luckily we had the skills to do it. We are told the kicker apologized, but we weren't there to hear it – we were chasing a mask before it drifted out of location range. Here is how to avoid kicking the next person on the back roll simultaneous entry:

1. Before you roll off, check your position, check the divers to your left and right.
2. If you are crowded ask nicely for a little space.
3. Move out of other divers' space.
4. Go at the same time as everyone else. That means get your stuff together and be ready to go when the dive master says go.

5. Just roll backwards. Don't push off or lunge. Just "fall in" by leaning backward and straightening your legs

6. When you feel wet move directly away from the boat

If you can't do this, then don't get on our boat, please. (Note: Debbie did kick a guy once, but it wasn't her fault. The other guy got in her space. Intolerable.)

Some people also kick, hit or jostle other people getting on and off the day boat, or moving around it. They kick, fall onto, elbow, head butt, or make other avoidable physical contact. These are selfish, oafish, unpleasant people who think the world revolves around them and who are totally mindless of anyone else's presence. They should have been drowned at birth. They are often late to arrive, late gearing up, probably smoke, and they usually don't have a boat bag. They move around cramped quarters oblivious to everyone else's comfort.

On the day boat, move slowly and deliberately. Hold onto something to keep from slipping or falling. Don't elbow past people. If you need someone to move, politely ask them to move. It's just good manners. You are not the only person on the boat. If you fall, you fall. If you fall on one of us, you do so at your peril.

TALK ONLY WHEN APPROPRIATE AND LIMIT YOURSELF TO PROPER CONTENT

On the day boat, it is ok to introduce yourself to other divers and ask where they are from. Polite greetings and exchanges are appropriate. If you lack a dive buddy, it is appropriate to ask others on the boat if they have a buddy and, if not, if they will buddy with you. But don't be a pest about it. We dive together as buddies on every dive when we are both on the boat. If we want more company, we will invite someone to join us. If you ask to join us and we don't want you to, we will turn you down politely, once.

After a dive, it is appropriate to share with others all the cool stuff you saw. That's why we all dive. It is also ok to report any symptoms of decompression sickness or other injury or problems. In fact, always do that. Polite, pleasant and positive conversation is always appropriate. Other stuff is not. Here is a list of conversation **don'ts:**

* **Don't bitch** at anyone on the boat, including your dive buddy, even if you are married to them.

* **Don't bitch** to or about anyone on the boat crew.

* **Don't bitch** about the weather, the visibility, currents, or anything else beyond the control of the people you paid to take your diving today.

* **Don't use profanity** at us or anyone else. Its bad manners.

* **Don't tell everyone** how your last dive here or elsewhere was so much better than this dive.

* **Don't talk so loud** that people not in your conversation end up being a part of it.

* **Don't offer unsolicited advice** to any other diver unless you are a licensed and insured divemaster or instructor and see the other person doing something dangerous and wrong. You have no doubt been on the boat with the person who has maybe 10 dives but can't stop telling people what to do and how to do it. And they are usually wrong. If someone asks you a question, and you are competent to answer or assist, then ok. But it might be more appropriate to direct them to a professional on board, preferably one who is being paid to work this particular dive outing.

* **Don't criticize other divers.** A Scuba Snob is allowed to criticize other divers, but really only does so on rare occasions. We prefer to talk about them after we have escaped from their presence. We hear husbands and wives speaking critically to each other before

and after dives. Sometimes a parent will yell at or be critical of a child. Sometimes it's a future ex-boyfriend criticizing his for-the-moment girlfriend.

When any of this happens, it can totally suck all the positive energy off of the boat, and even out of the surrounding ocean. One of the reasons we love diving is that the people are almost always fun. We can share the diving experience together, and it's all good. Until someone goes negative. Don't be that person.

Sadly, we have lived through too many examples of this to list, but you violators out there know who you are. If you do not qualify as a Scuba Snob, don't try and tell someone else how to set up their equipment, how to dive, or how to navigate the dive sight about to be explored.

I am sure that, like us, you have been on a dive boat where someone on board felt they knew it all, and insisted on sharing it. One time on a day boat off of Maui (it seems a lot of bad examples have happened there- maybe because we dive there a lot) we had one of these people on board. Conversation revealed that this was that person's second dive trip, and they last dove about a year earlier at some Caribbean location. After telling Dennis all about the best equipment to have (just like his), how to put on equipment once it was assembled, and showing off his ten inch dive knife, niftily strapped to the outside of his right calf (really), Dennis had enough, said thanks for sharing, and turned away. Of course, this was the diver who did not turn on his air, had inadequate weight to descend, and was generally a buzz kill for everyone on the dive.

PLEASE TIP

Do it. Tip something. Tip in local currency if you can. Always tip in cash. If you are clueless as to what is appropriate, then tip five to ten dollars per tank per diver.

That's a fair range. The tip can be on the lower end if the services provided are minimal, more if someone set up your gear for you, changed out your tank, gave you a beverage and/or snack and/or lunch. You should tip more if the divemaster retrieved the piece of gear you dropped overboard, or saved your life, or did something else special like that.

Some boats have a tip jar. We make a habit of asking if there is one, and usually ask loud enough so other people will hear us ask and hopefully tip. If there is a tip jar, put your entire tip in it. If there is none, tip the divemaster and captain separately. Also, tip every day since the crew and dive masters may change daily. But TIP.

Chapter 4

Liveaboard Rules Of Etiquette

A liveaboard is a big boat on which six to thirty-six divers eat, sleep, dive, and sometime bathe or shower together for three to ten days, or longer. The life style is a cross between living in a college dorm room, a jail cellblock, and a cabin at sleep away camp, but with lots of diving. All the day boat rules from Chapter 3 apply here too except for smoking and tipping. In those areas, the rules are different for a liveaboard and are discussed below.

Liveaboards vary tremendously in quality of accommodations, quality of meals, and, quite frankly, quality of clientele. Debbie has been on one liveaboard trip, and has no desire to repeat the experience because of the conduct of a few people. If there is "one of those" people on the trip, they can ruin it for everyone, and you cannot get away from them. We suppose you could maroon them on a deserted island, but the matter might then be in the courts for years. Dennis has been on several liveaboard trips. Based on cumulative experience, here are the truly important rules of etiquette for liveaboards, both on the boat and during land excursions.

FOLLOW THE RULES

Every liveaboard has safety briefings and sometimes fire drills. They also have rules and procedures for diving and logging off and on the boat, meal times and procedures, and rules regarding diving, such as time of day, no solo diving, and so on. Rules are unique to each boat and crew. Diving etiquette requires that you follow the rules. Everyone follows the same rules. Don't ask for a special rule for any reason, ever. If you need special rules, charter your own boat.

Dennis was once on a Caribbean liveaboard with 15 other divers a few years back, and one of the rules was "no solo diving." There was a 60-something female on board who had substantial experience and good diving skills, but she was a bitch. She was not on the trip with a buddy. (No surprise there!) No one wanted to dive with her, and she was nearly forbidden from diving at one point for breaking the "no solo diving" rule. Dennis, being the sweetheart that he is, agreed to dive with her late one afternoon. Dennis had already done five dives that day, and was on a pretty short no-decompression fuse even though the dive was planned to a maximum depth of only fifty feet. This limitation was shared with the one-time-only buddy as part of the dive planning. Off they went.

Upon approaching and then again upon reaching his no decompression limit, Dennis signaled to his buddy, the bitch, that it was time to surface. She wrote on her slate "go ahead, I have a lot of air left." So did Dennis- more than she had, in fact. That wasn't the point. Dennis's no decompression limits had been reached, and he had to surface or risk bad things happening. Dennis does not always carry a slate, but did on this occasion. He wrote back "We will both ascend now," held the slate to the bitch's face. He then gripped her buoyancy vest strap and ascended with her. (Sometimes the divemaster in Dennis comes out even when he is not officially working.)

On the dive deck, believing they were alone, the bitch went off on Dennis about everything, from touching her to telling her when a dive was over, to how everyone on the boat, including Dennis, sucked, everyone onboard was an asshole, etc. She had apparently forgotten that at that point on the trip Dennis was the only one willing to dive with her, a willingness that had now passed. The captain heard the exchange, and though there were two days of diving left, the bitch was done. The contract she had signed was clear. She had forfeited the right to dive, and got no refund. She didn't want to follow the rules, so she didn't get to play with the others.

No one saw her much after that. Although the rumors that the boat had a brig and she was locked in it were not true, it would have been appropriate. Follow the rules. Be nice. Get the full value of your trip.

KEEP YOUR STUFF OUT OF THE HALLWAYS AND COMMON AREAS

Everyone has a room assigned to them on a liveaboard. That is the place for your stuff. Your stuff does not belong in the corridor outside your room, or our room, or anywhere else in a corridor. People need to walk there. It may be a fire exit route. Keep it clear. Also, your stuff does not belong in the common areas unless you are using it. Your dive gear will also have an assigned area or locker. You use your space and we'll use ours and we can all be happy.

SMOKE ONLY IN DESIGNATED AREAS

If there is a designated smoking area, smoke there and nowhere else. Never smoke in the dining area or any common area not designated for smoking. Dispose of your butts as directed by the captain or crew. Pay attention to wind direction and stand down wind of others. If there is no designated smoking area on the boat, then feel free to smoke underwater but nowhere else.

USE ONLY YOUR FAIR SHARE OF FRESH WATER

Many, but not all, liveaboards have the capacity to purify sea water for drinking and other uses, but their capacities vary. There are still boats that do not have this technology at all. For that reason it is important to note the fresh water holding or producing capacity of the boat, factor in the number of guests plus crew, and *only use your fair share*. The crew will advise what that is by going over rules that everyone is to follow regarding fresh water use.

Dennis was on a boat with no fresh water producing capacity about ten years ago on a four day excursion to the Channel Islands off the coast of Southern California. Those that listened to the briefings heard that all divers were advised to take short showers and to not rinse their gear until the end of the trip. A fresh water bucket was available on the dive deck to rinse regulators and computers, and that was what was to be used. All of this seemed straight forward and simple. None the less, we ran out of fresh water in less than two days due to a party of four deciding they would rinse their gear in the shower *after every dive!* That included regulators, computers, buoyancy vests, and even wetsuits, for crying out loud. They also took long showers.

As a result, we all lost some dive time due to an unscheduled dockside stop to replenish the water supply. These people and there actions were rude, selfish, and gutless. Even worse, they were unrepentant. All the polite divers despised them. No doubt karmic justice has caught up with them by now.

Ask about fresh water capacity and use rules, and follow the directions of the boat crew. You are not the only person who has cool dive gear, or who needs to shower, or who might get thirsty. If you can't follow the rules like everyone else, don't get on the boat with us.

PRACTICE PROPER HYGIENE

Clean yourself. Wash up now and then. You know how funky dive gear can get. We divers get that funky too. Within the limits of the fresh water supply and any boat restrictions, please shower. Please change your clothes now and then. Also, before you wear a garment to a meal or to hang out in a common area with other people, make sure it passes the sniff test. Hold it up to your nose and inhale deeply. If you puke or pass out, please don't wear it and then sit next to us. If on giving it the sniff test you only feel nauseous, you still shouldn't wear it.

Dennis was on a liveaboard on which two young men brought exactly one shirt apiece for the entire trip. They slept in them, wore them constantly when not diving, and sometimes donned them when they were each still a little wet with sea water. By day three they smelled worse than cat vomit that has baked for three days in a car with closed windows. They didn't even air out the shirts during the day. We sometimes wonder if they had a clean shirt to wear on the plane ride home. Remember, it is more important to smell good than to look good when living in close quarters with 20 other people for several days. Please plan accordingly.

PRACTICE GOOD MANNERS DURING SHORE EXCURSIONS

This is the primary problem area that keeps Debbie from enjoying liveaboards. It can be bad enough being stuck on a boat for several days with someone who for some reason is just unpleasant to be around. But when there is a shore excursion where everyone still has to be together, sometimes things can actually get even worse. We were together on a liveabord in the eastern Caribbean a few years back, and there was a planned mini-bus tour of one of the islands. We decided to go. Bad call. The excursion included some very neat tours of an old cemetery and a museum, and some pretty spectacular 360 degree ocean views. Unfortunately, it also included a couple of shopping stops.

The first one was at a small local boutique, and one woman in our group insisted on spending over an hour there when everyone else was ready to go after a few minutes. She was a spoiled trophy wife who bitched regularly throughout the trip, and of course didn't think any rules applied to her. You know the type. Sitting around on the ground for 90 minutes waiting for someone to decide on a souvenir is not our idea of fun. When preparing for or going on a shore excursion from a liveaboard, we suggest these creative new rules should be followed:

* Before leaving on an excursion, all those who are planning to go ashore should line up on deck so each has a chance to look at the rest of the shore party and say "if (s)he's going, I'm not going."
* All who show up for a shore excursion should be allowed to, by majority vote, exclude up to 2 people from going.
* While ashore, remember it's a group thing. Do nothing to delay or hold up the group.
* Be on time for the trip back to the mother ship if you came ashore by launch, or be back on time if the mother ship is docked.
* If anyone in the shore party does not appear on the van or boat or bus within ten minutes of everyone else being onboard, they get left behind.
* Take your medication.

We are happiest when we are in a group of two or four. On rare occasions, we have actually enjoyed ourselves as part of a group of eight. Once. The chance of having a bad apple in a group increases dramatically as the size of the group increases. Don't be the bad apple. Don't be the person everyone wishes didn't come on the trip.

IF YOUR GEAR IS LATE, STAY CALM

It sometimes happens that you arrive by plane for a liveabord trip, but your gear does not. This happened to us. It was awful. The boat had to leave the island on which we landed before our gear arrived. We, as polite people, could not hold up the rest of the party, so off the boat went, with us aboard but without our gear. The next day, we missed nearly all of the diving. The boat had extra gear, and Dennis fashioned a prescription mask of sorts using the lenses from an extra pair of glasses. We learned from this experience to take as carry on any necessary unique equipment. For Dennis, that is a prescription lens dive mask.

If an airline delays your gear, don't blame the other divers on the trip. Don't blame the boat crew, either. Even if you feel miserable, put up a good front, and encourage the other divers to enjoy their dives. There is no need to make everyone else miserable. Ultimately, our gear made it aboard, and with several dive days left, we rapidly caught up to everyone else. If your gear is delayed, ask the crew if there is extra dive gear on board. There probably will be.

PLEASE TIP

Tipping is good manners and expected on every liveaboard. It is part of the income on which the crew depends. But is it just us, or do the expectation comments on the live- aboard brochures suggest really high tips? You should tip, and you should note in calculating your tip that you have been served all your meals, had dive deck services, maid service, and perhaps some medical care and photo/video services or equipment to use. Not only that, a qualified person drove the boat and you didn't sink or get lost. However, we don't think you necessarily need to tip the amount the brochures suggest, although you certainly can if you wish.

Ten dollars a day plus ten dollars a dive is pretty much our cap, absent extraordinary services. Do what you want, but do tip. Unless you were abandoned at a dive site by the boat. In that event you are excused from tipping.

Chapter 5

Dress Code

If you are with a group or if you will be visible to anyone other than yourself and your immediate family and/or really close friends, please bear in mind that while you don't have to see yourself, others have to see you. So exercise proper etiquette when it comes to dress. Here are our thoughts on the subject. These rules apply to dive boats, beaches, the dive resort, and every other public place.

The first and most obvious rule is this: no thong or bikini swimsuits for men. No man really looks good in these, and even if you think you do, a dive boat is not the proper venue. Most guys who wear them are not buff enough to look good in them, some are too heavy, and some are just too skinny and/or old. In such a case, tragedy can occur, and has. It struck on a beautiful March morning off the coast of Maui.

We were on a day boat during whale season, and were watching the humpbacks as we motored to the dive sight. On the boat there was a very fun group from Germany together with an assortment of us Americans. One of the Germans was a man about seventy years of age who was wearing a bikini swim suit that he quite clearly purchased years earlier when his thighs carried more muscle. The leg openings on the suit were a lot bigger than his legs. Consequently, when he turned and stepped abruptly to cross to the opposite side of the boat in order to see the whales, his package fell out of the wrapper. He, of course, didn't notice immediately, and no one seemed too comfortable in talking to him at that point. Our excuse was that we didn't speak German.

The man geared up for the dive, but did not put on a wetsuit, just a shirt. The rest of him remained uncovered. During his descent it looked like he had a small remora latched to his crotch. It was not a pretty sight. No bikinis or thongs on the guys, please. Not even if you are from Europe. Also, wear a suit that fits.

Women should also wear bathing suits that fit. Not too loose, not too tight. Debbie says bikinis are ok for women if they look good in the bikini. Dennis can live with that rule. However, ladies, who is to say if you look good or not? On this rule all of you are on the honor system. We are confident you will make good choices. We are less confident your men will make good choices, so please, inspect the swimwear your men propose to wear and make necessary changes and corrections.

Another rule for the guys is not to sag too far. Again, it's not the venue. Showing your butt crack on a dive boat where we are often pressed close together is just not right. We don't want your butt crack in our face, and you don't want Dennis's in yours.

Some of us, and we know who we are, need to wear a shirt or other cover-up when on the boat. Some of you don't. Some of you think you don't, but you do. How to tell? Take a picture of yourself wearing only your swimsuit. Then cover up the head in the photograph. Now show it someone close to you, like a spouse or coworker. If they spontaneously laugh, scream, puke or pass out, you should cover up on the boat. It's just good manners.

Another dress code rule is that you should not wear a shirt, sweats, cover-up or other clothing that has profane or provocative writing. Be family friendly. Avoid crude, sexist or racist words or pictures as well. Political statements are a tough call, but since it seems that all the meaningful political statements include profanity or sexist overtones, leave those home too. That leaves all the cool shirts from places you have been diving or hope to dive. College jerseys work too. So does clothing with no writing. Really.

Some people think that wet suit and fin colors should follow certain rules. Dennis once did, but no more. Paisley, neon, and weird color combinations are fine. We prefer black and dark grey, but let's face it: Dennis went through his lime green phase and Debbie went through a (very short) pink phase. Some of our best friends and favorite dive buddies actually have colors on their gear. So make a statement. Be accepting of others. At least when you are on the boat with them. You can make fun of them later.

Chapter 6

Underwater Etiquette

$\mathcal{E}$very rule in this book is important, but the rules in this chapter are the most important of all. That is because now we are talking about how to behave when you are actually diving, or more specifically, when you are diving *near us*.

DON'T CHASE ANYTHING

You will never catch up to anything in the ocean by chasing it. This includes sea creatures and other divers. You will drive them away. If there is an interesting creature nearby and you want to get closer, start by stopping. Observe the animal. Plan an indirect approach, if you are going to approach at all. Then approach slowly. Break off the approach if the animal shows by its actions it is going to move away or if looks like it is going to eat you.

There is a wonderful dive site on Maui called Olawalu. You have our permission and encouragement to dive it. There is beautiful hard coral, an abundance colorful fish and lots of green sea turtles. You can dive this site from the shore or from a boat. It is great either way and is accessible year round. One time when we were diving this site from a day boat on which there was a total of eight divers, Debbie and I found ourselves kneeling in the sand about 45 feet down when three very large turtles emerged and started swimming in slow and slowly ascending circles around us, no more than perhaps ten feet from us at any time. We calmly ascended very slowly, back to back, and joined in this turtle dance - for about five seconds. Then the "scuba idiot" spotted us. He was about twenty yards away, standing on a coral head (an indication of his lack of skills and etiquette). He charged us and the turtles, the turtles fled, and what was about to be the experience of a lifetime evaporated instantly.

This person, who will forever be the "scuba idiot" in our book, was, in fact, the same guy who dumped his massive gear trunk on the dive platform mentioned in Chapter 3. There he was again. No boat bag, no skills, no class, no manners. Whoever you are, I hope you are reading this book. You really need it. **Don't chase anything. Ever.**

On the topic of chasing things, Debbie insists on mentioning an episode off the coast of Grand Cayman as another example. It involved Dennis. Debbie *claims* Dennis chased after a turtle to get some video. Dennis would never chase after a turtle, though. What really happened, according to Dennis, is that he swam *alongside* a young hawksbill and got terrific video. The turtle went behind and between soft corals and hard corals, the light was perfect, and no one else was around to get in the frame. This was at the end of a long and relatively deep dive, and air supply was an issue. (Thank you, Debbie, for sharing at the safety stop. Love, Dennis) Maybe Debbie was right, and karmic justice prevailed when Dennis inadvertently erased the best three minutes of video he ever took. If he hadn't erased it, he could prove he wasn't chasing. He was swimming alongside, eyeball to eyeball. But the rule is the rule. Don't chase anything. Ever. Not even if you are a qualified Scuba Snob.

DON'T CROWD

Have you ever seen something really interesting on a dive, only to have another diver or five rush to your location, push in front of you, and screw up the moment and the photo you hoped to take? They probably also kicked up the bottom or the wall and totally screwed up the visibility, too. It's pretty likely you have had this happen. If not, then you have probably been a perpetrator. Dive buddies should always be in touching distance of each other with few exceptions. Everyone else, please back the hell off!

If you see us or anyone else looking at something or pointing or taking a photo and you are curious, then approach slowly. Hang out for a bit about four to six feet above us and at least six feet behind us. Wait for us, or whoever, to clear the location. Then take your turn. Is that so hard? Didn't we learn to take turns from our mommies or daddies, or our kindergarten teacher? Come on people, let's take turns under water, too.

One time in Mexico we were diving with a man about our age who was shooting video on every dive. He had over 1000 dives and excellent scuba skills, including great buoyancy control. Too bad he had no manners. Every time a turtle or barracuda or ray approached us, regardless of where he was, he charged the creature, took video until it swam off, and acted like this was just fine. Well it wasn't. He actually kicked Dennis on one mad dash to get to the object of his video quest. After that happened we did not dive with him any more. Sadly, we have even had the misfortune of local divemasters acting out this way. There is no rule that says the divemaster has to see every cool thing before anyone else does. Please don't crowd, don't monopolize, and don't be a jerk. It's not necessary. It's a big ocean out there with enough neat stuff for everyone to see and get close too.

STAY OFF THE REEF

So everyone knows to stay off the reef, right? We were reminded of this rule in every scuba class we ever took, and probably every briefing before a boat dive. Unfortunately, some people out there don't listen to the briefings or else think they don't have to be careful to not destroy precious, beautiful, fragile and endangered coral. Staying off the reef means don't stand on it, don't hold onto it, don't stab it with your dive knife, and don't let your computer, submersible pressure gauge, or alternate air source dangle and hit it. Everybody- if you see someone violating this rule- PLEASE, confront them, help them make an immediate correction. If they do not correct by themselves, then you might think of a way to make them correct. (Though turning off their air might be a little extreme, and is in fact never appropriate. Dammit.)

DON'T KICK UP THE BOTTOM

If it's a sandy bottom, feel free to lie down, sit or kneel. We once rested quietly on a sandy bottom for a very long time communing with a grouper who ultimately moved to within about 18 inches of us. But even a sandy bottom can be kicked up and the visibility dropped to zero. This is especially true in confined areas like swim-throughs. Debbie loves a good swim-through as much as anyone. She likes caves too. Dennis is less enthusiastic, but still enjoys them. However, no one can enjoy a swim-through when following a diver who, although not technically touching the bottom, kicks it up with their fin kicks. Here are some way to avoid kicking up the bottom:

a)   Stay higher off the bottom. For some of you, about ten feet should do it.

b)   Keep your feet and fins higher than your head.

c)   Try using a gentle frog kick.

d)   Move slower.

e)   Look back between your legs now and then. This move will not only let you see if you are kicking up the bottom, it will also cause your feet and fins to elevate and, if you are kicking up the bottom, will allow you to see the diver behind you flipping you off.

DON'T DANGLE

Here's another thing we all learned on our first open water dive or before: Don't let stuff dangle. That means your gauges, alternate air source, camera, collection bag, dive lights- anything clipped to you. Secure it all so it doesn't drag and damage the reef, catch and entangle on a buddy's buoyancy vest. (yes, we've seen this happen), or even cause you to hang yourself when doing a back roll entry. If you are renting equipment, insist on having a place to secure everything. If you own your own gear, we suggest retractors for securing gauge consoles. And if you're a skinny guy in a bikini with worn out elastic, don't let your "package" dangle, either. (See discussion in Chapter 5.)

LOOK AT YOUR GAUGES REGULARLY

Ok divers, listen up. Before we go on our next dive, let's review some basics. Running off of your first stage (that thing connected to your tank of compressed air) there are four hoses. One is a low pressure inflater hose attached to your buoyancy vest. The second hose goes to your primary regulator so you can breathe under water. The third goes to your alternate air source (unless you have a low pressure inflater alternate air source set up) so someone else can breathe off your tank in an emergency. Finally, the fourth hose goes to your submersible pressure gauge and maybe to your computer, what we will call your "console." That is what we are talking about here, the gauge console at the end of the fourth hose. (We get it- some of you have wrist mounted integrated, no hose computers and stuff- fine. Quit interrupting).

As to the stuff at the end of the fourth hose, (or on your wrist mount) *look at it* now and then! Some people never look at their gauges, believe it or not. You should look at your gauges before your dive and see if you have sufficient air for the dive. You can look at it during the dive and you will see how much air you have left. Isn't that something? Look at your computer or gauge during the dive and it will tell you how deep you are. Look at your computer and you will actually see how much no decompression time you have left at the depth you are at! No joke! It's amazing! So please, look at your gauges!

Why watch your gauges? For your safety and the safety of those around you. We all want to enjoy the dive, and we want you to enjoy the dive too. If your air is limited, please consider reducing your depth by ten feet or so you won't make us all go up because you are low on air. To know where you stand on air, or how deep your are, YOU NEED TO LOOK AT YOUR CONSOLE! It's part of good diving etiquette. Doing so will help reduce the times other divers have to retrieve you from unsafe depths, or escort you to the dive boat as you suck the air from our tank (which we will share willingly if needed) because you didn't pay attention to your air supply. Keeping an eye on your gauges will also enhance you awareness generally, which leads to better diving skills.

We shudder when we hear a diver after a dive ask "How deep did we go?" or "How long were we down?" Sometimes they will look at their computer for the first time after the dive and say "WOW, I didn't know I went that deep!" These people are disasters waiting to happen. A distressed diver can be a hazard to those who try to assist them. Be a safe diver. Be aware. Look at your #%!**+ gauges! Read them often. Live to dive another day.

FOLLOW THE DIVE PROFILE PLANNED

To do this, you need to read your #%!**+ gauges! (See above.) If you dive with a group, stay with the group. If the dive is planned to a maximum depth of 90 feet, don't go 100 feet. It's ok to go shallower, but not deeper, especially on repetitive dives. Following the dive profile includes following the time as well as depth limits.

Even though we are almost always the last ones on the boat (a big deal for Debbie- she keeps "first in last out statistics), we stick to the time directives if they have been established for the dive. We often dive on our own, just the two of us. In those cases we set **and follow** our own profile. We plan our dive and dive our plan. Ever heard that one before? But in a group, we follow the group dive plan, and so do all competent and well mannered divers. If you can't do that, you can't dive with us. Or anyone else. Ever.

AVOID BEING AN AIR SUCKER

We really don't care how you are on air unless you are diving with us. Swim a mile in ten minutes, go deep, don't trim your weighting for the conditions, we don't care. But if you are diving with us, in our group, then we do care. Not everyone uses up their air at the same rate. We get that. But some people are terrible and don't need to be. Some air suckage is correctable. You can, through good diving practices, reduce your air consumption. Here are some tips for you air suckers to improve your bottom time:

a) Check your weighting. If you go through air faster

than everyone else, there is a real good chance you are over-weighted or under-weighted.

b) Trim your buoyancy often. We regularly observe other divers and see that they cannot hover. To remain at a certain depth, they are kicking or moving their arms to maintain that depth. Those movements burn air. Use your low pressure inflater/ deflater- that is what it is there for. Maintain neutral buoyancy and you will use a lot less air.

c) Move less. Swim less. Stop and smell the coral. Look for pretty little things under ledges. Don't be in constant motion.

d) Stay a few meters above the rest of the group.

If you will do these four things, we are confident that you will suck less air, and for some of you, a lot less air. Even though we don't all consume air at the same rate, being an air sucker is not good diving etiquette because you may cause the rest of us to have to cut short our dive. That can be a real pisser. Consider the lady on a dive boat off Molokai.

This was an adventurous, high stress hammerhead shark dive, 90 feet deep, strong currents, with special entry and exit rules because there was no mooring and the boat was at the mercy of ten foot high waves. In addition to all of that, we had an hour long boat ride to get the site, and it was a very rough ride. Dennis puked more than once. On arrival at the dive site we were all anxious to make the dive. Most of us listened to the briefing about current, depth, where to look for the hammerheads, and so on. Most of us. But one diver, "the lady," was clueless. About 14 minutes into the dive, just when we first sighted a nice school of hammerheads, the lady signaled low on air. Actually she was way beyond low, and because of conditions, the dive came to an end for everyone. After fourteen minutes, and she was down to about 400 psi in her tank. Everyone else had at least four times that much. The lady was the buzz killer. She cheated the rest of us out of our dive. Why do we say it was her fault? Because it was! She swam around like a crazy person the entire time; she didn't listen to the briefing and so hung in the strongest part of the current; she had negligible buoyancy control; she was clearly overweighted (and overweight); she was not qualified to do the dive and so was anxious the entire time. She also didn't monitor her gauges or she would have known that for most of the dive she was ten feet or more deeper than the profile planned, and she never corrected for that. It's a miracle she looked at her gauges before her air was totally depleted!

The lady was not allowed to do the second dive. She should never have been on the first dive. She misrepresented her experience and competence. While she was joking about getting a t-shirt that said "I survived the Molokai Shark Dive," everyone else on the boat was wishing she hadn't. No one has to be an air sucker. We can all do a little better. Come on people, work on your skills!

DON'T FEED ANYTHING TO ANYTHING THAT LIVES IN THE OCEAN

We feel very strongly about this. The only real exception is if you puke in the ocean because that is really a part of the ecosystem. We don't go on shark dives where the concessionaire feeds the sharks. We don't feed frozen peas to fish or eels. We don't smear squeeze cheese on mermaid statues to get the fish to look like they are kissing the mermaid. We have seen all of these things done. While we have to admit that the cheese on the mermaid at Sunset Reef in Grand Cayman was pretty cool, with large grey angelfish looking like they were kissing her on the lips, it was still wrong. If you feel differently, we won't dive with you, and you can never be a Scuba Snob.

Dennis fed the fish inadvertently once on a dive off of Lanai, and not by puking. Focusing on taking a photo, he swam into the side of a lava tube and gashed his head pretty deeply. He bled a lot. It looked like an ink cloud from an octopus, but apparently it was less noxious because every little butterfly fish and yellow tang within a mile descended on him. He looked like he was in the middle of a swarm of bees. If you really want to feed the fish, go ahead and open up a vein. But other than that (and puking), if you are with a Scuba Snob, there is no fish feeding.

STAY WITH YOUR BUDDY, STAY WITH YOUR GROUP

How basic a rule is this? Yet, not everyone gets it. We were on a dive in Cozumel one time when a casual diver with less than ideal skills cut away from the group and descended way below the planned depth for the dive. He was also swimming here and there and clearly burning through his air at an alarming rate. Dennis followed him while Debbie positioned herself so she could keep both them and the rest of the group in sight. Dennis tapped on the diver's shoulder, pointed upward toward the group which was about fifty feet overhead and quite a way off to the north. The diver's anger at being contacted was visible even behind his mask, but he did come along after a short detour when Dennis had to descend to retrieve a weight pocket that Mr. Wonderful dropped in his jerky moving about.

At the end of the dive, which was short (because guess who ran out of air) the diver really got in Dennis's face. After we let him rant for a moment, it was his own dive buddy (using the term loosely because the subject diver was 100 feet away from him during most of the dive) who said that he should be thanking us, not expressing anger at us. Thank you! By the way, we talked about him the rest of the week. As Scuba Snobs, we were allowed. We didn't have to

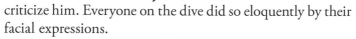

criticize him. Everyone on the dive did so eloquently by their facial expressions.

Debbie thinks it is appropriate here to reiterate the alleged turtle chase allegation from the first rule in this chapter. She also wanted to add to it a recent episode in Mexico involving Dennis and a sting ray where Dennis allegedly swam away from Debbie suddenly and without notice, but Dennis thinks that would be redundant and boring.

Chapter 7

Special Rules of Etiquette for Night Diving

If you have not yet experienced the ocean at night, we highly recommend it. You can see creatures and behaviors not normally seen during the day. The whole experience is fantastic. There are just a few special rules of etiquette that apply to night dives, together with all of the rules of Chapter 6. Chapter 6 rules need to be applied very strictly to night dives. Here are few more rules of etiquette to remember and to practice when diving at night:

USE A TANK LIGHT

Have a tank light. That's a light you attach to your tank to make yourself more visible. These can be any color. Some flash, some look like luminous pencils. Anything will work, but it needs to be battery powered. **No chemical sticks**. They are an absolute terror on the environment above and below water, please.

HAVE ONE OR MORE GOOD DIVE LIGHTS

It's not just safety, it's good manners. Have a good light, preferably two, and check the power level before the dive. We each make certain to have two functioning and well-charged lights on every night dive, and even then there is not guarantee. On a night dive off of Statia a few years back we entered with two lights apiece. We checked them all, they had new batteries. Within ten minutes, for whatever reason, we were down to one. OOPS!!! We were alone on this dive, so we salvaged it by remaining close to the boat and limiting the duration of the dive. This is not fun. Fortunately, we didn't screw up anyone else's dive, just our own. We switched dive light brands after that episode.

CONTROL THE BEAM OF YOUR DIVE LIGHT

Don't shine your light in our eyes. This is really an important rule. It doesn't matter if you do it on purpose as a joke or because you don't like us or just do it by accident. It is always bad manners and dangerous, too. Diving is a visual sport and temporary blindness can cause the affected diver to mistake you for an attacker or terrorist, and they might spear, stab, kick or hit you. Maintain control of your light, and shine it away from others.

TAKE A COMPASS, USE A COMPASS

On a night dive, you should a) have a compass, b) know how to use it, and c) use it. Let's face it, in good visibility and plenty of light navigation is usually not an issue. At night it is always an issue. Knowing where you are is important to your safety and is a courtesy to those who will have to come and find you in the dark if you get lost. If you are not comfortable on your own on a night dive, you can come with us if you ask nicely and stay with the group. Debbie is not a compass person, but she has one on her console.

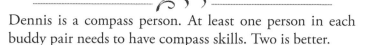

Dennis is a compass person. At least one person in each buddy pair needs to have compass skills. Two is better.

STAY TOGETHER

If you are in a group, stay with the group and close to the group. Always. If there is a designated leader, and there should be, follow the leader. You can come with us if you do these things. If you don't, you can't come with us on a night dive ever again. Probably. Unless you loan us a real good light if ours go out. Then maybe.

Chapter 8

Punctuality- the Ultimate Expression of Good Manners

Just when we thought we were about to wrap up this important little book, we realized that we had not emphasized punctuality nearly enough. It has cropped up a little here and there, but it is an important rule of etiquette in every aspect of life and in every aspect of diving. The only skill you need to be punctual is the ability to tell time. Most of us learned that before the age of eight. There is no acceptable excuse for being late, ever.

First, be punctual when meeting at the dive center or dock. If the plan is to depart at 8:00 a.m., don't show up to check in at 8:00 a.m. Show up as early as you need to in order to do paperwork, acquire any gear you do not have with you, and ask all the questions you can dream up. You need to be done with all of that *before* 8:00 a.m. Otherwise, just stay home. Making people wait on you because you cannot get it together is a serious offense against the dive community.

Next, be punctual in arriving at any form of transportation you are sharing with others. That means being there *ready to climb aboard at departure time*. Once in Mexico we signed up for a dive at a remote location. We were told to be at the van with our gear at 1:00 p.m. All but one person was there. That person wandered up over a half hour later. Not only was that bad manners on his part, it also wasn't too polite that the dive shop made us all wait for him.

Once you show up on time, stay around, please. That is part of punctuality, too. One day on Grand Cayman our dive boat could not depart from the nearby dock due to wind conditions. Because of that, when we arrived for the dive the shop had a truck for gear and a van to take us on a 10 minute drive to the south shore where we could dive. No problem. Everyone could load their gear and climb on the van and off we would go without delay. So we thought. No such luck. Three of the divers in the group felt this was a reason to run errands or wander off to fill their water bottle, to run back to the room for some unimportant thing, or even to go pee. Off they went while all of us polite people waited in a van. It was hot, we were anxious to go, yet we sat there waiting for these others to decide to board. When Dennis suggested we take off without them, some on the van thought that would be rude. Rude is what those three were. Don't be like them.

Be punctual in getting ready to begin a dive. Get your gear set up. Check it, fix what needs fixing, ask for help if you need it. Do this so that when the divemaster says "the pool is open," you can proceed to the dive deck and plunge in. There are some divers who wait until the last minute to set up and get ready. These are the same people you cuss at in the grocery store because they wait for the cashier to give them a total before they even start looking for their checkbook. Punctuality is a constant requirement. Be ready to go, whatever "go" means, on time, when everyone else is ready.

Finally, if you are diving on a day boat or liveaboard where individual buddy teams are allowed to dive their own profiles but with a set return time for everyone, be punctual about returning to the boat. If the boat recalls divers by pre-arranged signal, be punctual in returning, Recalls rarely happen, but when they do there is a really good reason for them. Conditions on the sea can change, someone might be hurt, or something else has compelled the early recall. Be punctual returning to the boat by a prearranged time or in the event of a recall. It's important, and it's good manners.

Our daughter reminds us that if you are shore diving and have a shore person or group waiting and watching for you, return by the time you say you will return, and in that same place. We have to confess we were diving off shore on Maui one time and were later returning than we told our daughter we would be. We also returned a couple of hundred meters away from the prearranged exit point. We did meet up with our daughter, but just barely before she went off to alert the Coast Guard. She pointed out our errors to us in very clear terms, and she was right. Our bad. That was almost eight years ago. We learned from our mistake, and have not repeated it. We hope she will forgive us soon.

Chapter 9

Après Dive Rules

After the dive, or more accurately after the day's diving is done, there is a transitional period before we all are cleaned up and rehydrated with a few local brews. It is that time interval to which these après dive rules apply.

RINSE YOUR GEAR IN THE PROPER PLACE

Don't rinse your wetsuit in the same rinse tank as buoyancy vests and regulators. You peed in your wetsuit and I peed in mine. Rinse your wet suit with a hose or in a fresh water shower or the shower in your room. Keep your pee out of our stuff, and we'll keep our pee out of your stuff. It's just good manners.

Don't jump in a swimming pool with any dive gear on that you just wore in the ocean. Our friend Derek who owns Underwater Phantaseas in Lakewood, Colorado (the finest dive center in the nation, through which you can acquire this book and who we now expect to give us discounts on everything we buy) reminded us of the need to emphasize this rule. We totally agree. We call this the "Cozumel Fallacy." It seems in Cozumel more than anywhere else, people will get off a dive boat, walk down the dock, and jump into the swimming pool or even the hot tub with their pee- saturated wet suits on, and sometimes even with their buoyancy vests and regulators and everything else. Even local divemasters have been seen to do this on occasion. This is wrong. This is not tolerable. This is a mortal sin. Maybe even a capital crime. If you do this, shame on you. If you do this when we are in the pool or the hot tub, a curse be on you. If you see someone do this, yell at them and report them to the staff of the hotel and dive boat. Then call the consulate and do what you must to get them deported from the country immediately.

LEAVE THE BOAT IN AN EFFICIENT AND ORDERLY MANNER

Get your gear. Put it in your boat bag. Move off the boat in an orderly fashion. Do not linger, but do not shove and push either. Once off the boat, pick up all your stuff from the dock and walk away from the boat. Once you have moved clear of the only walkway we all have to use, you may drop your stuff, have a seat, light a cigarette if you must, and spread out. Do not stand on the dock right where the exit is and chit chat with your friends or the boat crew. Do not leave your stuff on the dock where we might trip over it. It is a Scuba Snob rule that anything we trip over on the dock is ours. Do not test us on this. Ok, if you do we probably won't keep your stuff, but it just might get kicked off the side of the dock.

Does that sound mean? It's not mean. Mean is stopping when you should be moving. Mean is creating hazards for sweet older people like us. Get your stuff, get off the boat, move off the dock. We promise to do the same.

LOGGING DIVES

You should log all of your dives. You can ask us to sign your log book, and we will. We love to sign log books, and have you sign ours. We each have a cool stamp with our name, certification, and a cool little picture- turtle for Debbie, sea horse for Dennis. If this book catches on we might get even cooler stamps and even stickers. And we will still sign your book. We're Scuba Snobs, not snobs.

There is no specific time and place to fill out your log book, but there are times and places not to do it. Don't do it while other people are waiting for you to move out of their way. Don't do it in the head on the boat. Don't do it during a pre-dive briefing. If someone else is logging their dive, stand back if you are wet so that you will not drip on their log book. Never grab someone's log book while they are logging their dives. If you need to copy data from our log books, ask first and we will be happy to share. Grab at them, though, and we won't.

A lot of people wait until quite a while after a dive to log it, getting data off their computer, or copying out of their dive buddy's log book. That's ok. Debbie does that. The important point is that Scuba Snobs log all their dives. In a book. With real pages. Using ink. A log book is a book, not a "file." It's ok if you keep your dive log on a computer, it just doesn't count as logging your dives. You should also have a real log book with pages. You need a real log book so you can fill it with lots of cool stamps and stickers from dive shops around the world, from the liveaboards you've been on, and from us. Did we mention we have cool stamps ? Also, you need a log book for people to sign off on your dives, and for interesting people to write down their contact information. You can also write in it good and bad things that happened on a dive so you have a record of them in case you are going to write a book like this one day

Chapter 10

Dive Talking

Although we have discussed this issue a little bit in Chapter 3, there is more to be said about dive conversation. Talking about diving is fun. Not as fun as diving, but still fun. Talking about diving with other divers is one way we learn of new dive sites and dive destinations. It is also how we get new people interested in diving. Most people can talk pretty well, but when you are talking diving, there are some rules of etiquette to be followed.

TALK WITHIN YOUR LIMITS

Just as you should dive within your limits, you need to talk within your limits too. Talk about your actual experiences. There is something to say about every dive. You don't need to embellish. If you do you will be found out, unless you are really good at it, as discussed below. When Dennis first began diving, and had returned from his first trip, he mentioned the fact to a client of his. The client congratulated him and told him that he too was a diver.

Dennis asked him where he had dove, and his answer was that he recently dove the Bahamas. As a newbie, Dennis then asked a newbie question. "How deep have you been?" Why do we always ask that as new divers? Anyway, the client said, and this is absolutely true, "Oh, I don't know, maybe six hundred feet." *Busted!* For you non-divers, let me explain. The recreational dive limit is 130 feet. Some technical diving is done two or three times that deep, by maybe a couple of hundred people in the world. To say you dove to six hundred feet is like saying you have high jumped thirty feet, or run a one minute mile. Don't talk about what you don't know. Stick to what you know and have experienced. That's good enough.

When you speak of dive destinations you have been to, make it clear when or how often you have been there and the extent of your experience there. If you were on a cruise and did two dives off Grand Cayman one day, you are not qualified to tell everyone what the best dive sites there are. Don't say "If you're going to Grand Cayman you've got to do Eden Rock and Sting Ray City. Those are the best dives there." What you should say is " I dove Grand Cayman. I was on a cruise ship and only got to dive two sites. They were both good, though. We did Sting Ray City and Eden Rock." What's wrong with that? Nothing. If people who are headed there want more information, they will ask you. On the other hand, if the others in the conversation have been to Grand Cayman several times and have dove dozens of different sites, they will know you are full of it, and you will make a fool of yourself. We are just trying to help here.

ONLY TELL LIES WHEN THEY ARE REALLY GOOD AND WELL TOLD

We were once told that the difference between a good dive story and a fairy tale is this: A fairy tale starts "Once

upon a time,…". A dive story starts "Now this is no shit…."
There are in fact some good dive stories that are, well, lies.
Or works of fiction. They are still good stories, and it's ok
to tell them. But before you do, make sure you follow these
rules:

1) Take your time to develop a good story. Don't try to
   tell one extemporaneously. That never works. Create
   the plot line, invent interesting details, and rehearse
   the story many times before telling it to someone
   else.

2) If you "borrow" facts for the story from the experiences
   of other divers, note who they are so you don't tell the
   story to them or in their presence.

3) Good stories have details. Lots of details. Include
   weather conditions, describe wet suit color, and
   certainly knife size and color. What was the depth,
   the lighting, the viz. Don't forget the weather, and
   what people were wearing. Details make lies come
   alive.

4) Make a little joke on yourself when appropriate. It
   shows confidence and self assurance.

5) A good story is never complete. There is always another
   detail to add. Never be satisfied. Strive for perfection.
   Make your story better in every retelling.

Dennis tells a story he has been developing for years.
He told it on a liveaboard one time in the late night hours
after a night dive, when there were just two other people
and quite a few beer bottles there to hear it. It was and is a
great story, mostly true, about a guy who was startled by a
large green moray that a group of divers had been feeding
unbeknownst to the star of the story. The feeders ran out
of food, so the moray went elsewhere looking for a handout
and headed toward the oblivious diver. That diver turned,
saw a six foot long moray swimming right at him, pulled

out his trusty dive knife, and stabbed at the eel. He missed the eel but hit himself in the right leg plunging the knife in very deeply, and had to be rushed to medical care. Properly told, the story is worth about thirty to forty minutes if you are sure to include all the relevant and irrelevant details and embellishments.

So Dennis told the story. The very next day at breakfast, when Dennis went to breakfast, there was one of the audience members from the previous evening telling the story as his own to divers who hadn't heard the telling the night before. This story thief was telling the story as if he had been there. How rude! And Dennis was standing right there! Plus, the story thief did a terrible job of telling the story. He rushed it, leaving out all the creative details. If you appropriate another diver's story, at least have the courtesy to only tell it when they are not around. And do it justice.

KNOW WHEN TO GIVE AND NOT GIVE ADVICE

Another important rule of dive conversation etiquette is to know when to give advice. *The only proper time to give advice is when you are asked for it*, and then *only if you are competent to provide the information requested*. If another diver asks you what qualities you look for in a regulator, they are asking your opinion and anyone can offer their opinion freely. As an opinion. If they ask you what regulator is the best and you have owned and used exactly one regulator in your dive lifetime, you are not competent to answer unless you limit your answer to saying, " I have only ever used an XYZ regulator, but I have been very happy with it." It's like having two dives in the Caymans – you're not an expert on regulators, but you can share what you know.

Do not give unsolicited advice to other divers on the dive boat. Ever. Not even if you are a bona fide Scuba Snob. The only exception is that if you are a currently licensed and

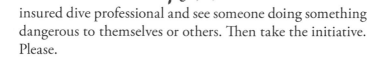

insured dive professional and see someone doing something dangerous to themselves or others. Then take the initiative. Please.

KNOW WHEN TO STOP TALKING

Knowing when to stop talking (*Dennis!*) is as important as knowing what to say and how to say it. Take a breath every now and then. Let someone else contribute. Every diver has a cool dive experience to share. Let them

Even more importantly, if you end up in a conversation with others you dove with and you were the reason a dive was short or crappy because of inferior skills or whatever, you do not need to apologize. You should not try to explain. Just be quiet. True Scuba Snobs will leave you alone for an appropriate interval, and then forget about it. At least in your presence. There is no conversation that will make it better. Use the time you would have spent apologizing to start creating a good story, making light of yourself but focusing on the lesson you learned that made you a better diver. Then tell that story.

Chapter 11

Apology

We're sorry. We probably offended someone in the dive world with our little book. We're especially sorry if it was you. We Scuba Snobs are ambassadors of our sport, encouraging others to join us, encouraging those who are already divers to be better divers, in word and by example. It is a heavy burden and an important mission. It can be stressful and lead to sarcasm, even occasional profanity. But let's face it, sometimes you just have to call an asshole an asshole. Or a bitch a bitch. We do it out of love. We mean it in a good way.

Scuba diving is serious fun. That means it's really, really, really, really fun. It also means that it is a serious venture, and to have fun you need to be safe. You need to be seriously engaged. You need proper equipment, proper training, and necessary skills. You need to keep those skills tuned and your equipment tuned. Every diver should be a Scuba Snob. Remember, a Scuba Snob is an avid and active diver who loves everything about diving and who has worked hard to acquire and maintain competent diving skills and good diving habits. They exercise and demonstrate those skills and habits when diving, and expect other divers to do the same.

Thanks for reading our book. Thanks for not hating us. Let's be friends. Here's an idea- Let's go diving!

Chapter 12

Take the Scuba Snobs Quiz

This brief quiz should be taken once you have finished Chapters One through Eleven. Your score will reveal all of the following:

  a) whether you can read
  b) whether you can remember what you read
  c) whether you can spot sarcasm and irony and understand it for what it is
  d) whether you can take a joke
  e) whether you might be Scuba Snob material.

You will be glad to know that all questions are multiple choice. You will also be glad to know that this is an open book quiz. It is also pass / fail. Now, the quiz:

1. On a day boat, where is it appropriate to pee?
    a) off the side of the boat when no one is looking
    b) in the camera bucket
    c) on the deck if you leave your wetsuit on
    d) none of the above

2. If you are on a dive and see another diver standing on the coral reef, you should:
   a) join them
   b) shoot them with your spear gun
   c) turn off their air
   d) none of the above

3. Which of the following are appropriate for a male diver to wear on a dive boat?
   a) a thong swimming suit
   b) a t-shirt with a picture of a naked woman on it
   c) sagged jams revealing a little bit of butt crack
   d) none of the above

4. What is the proper amount to tip on a day boat?
   a) if Dennis is the divemaster, $100.00 per person
   b) normally, $5.00 to $10.00 per dive depending on level of service
   c) if the boat abandoned you at a dive site, zero
   d) all of the above

5. On a liveaboard, the "sniff test" refers to:
   a) checking your roommate's pits for body odor
   b) determining if the head is occupied
   c) evaluating the edibility of some new food item
   d) none of the above

6. When/how often should you look at your gauges?
    a) at the beginning and ending of the dive only
    b) only after the dive to get data to log the dive
    c) gauges? We don't need no stinkin' gauges!
    d) none of the above

7. Which of the following are proper places to rinse a wetsuit?
    a) a fresh water shower at the beach or dock
    b) the shower in your hotel room or condo
    c) a rinse tank marked "rinse your wetsuit here"
    d) all of the above

8. Which of the following people are NOT required to follow the rules on a liveabord ?
    a) currently certified and insured instructors and divemasters
    b) people over the age of 55
    c) people from California
    d) none of the above

9. Your can reduce air consumption and avoid being an air sucker by doing which of the following?
    a) make sure you are weighted properly
    b) trimming your buoyancy often
    c) staying a few meters above other divers in the group
    d) all of the above

10. Your next dive trip is:
    a) tomorrow
    b) on the calendar and coming up soon
    c) just a dream; I don't when I'll get to dive again
    d) I'm so inspired by this book I'm going to plan it now!

The correct answer for each question is d), but on number 10 you get credit for any answer except c. If you said c, we feel bad for you, but you still don't get credit.

A passing grade is 10 out of 10. Anything less than that is failing. If you failed, take heart. Remember, the quiz is just about what we think. We're right, of course, but still.

SERIOUSLY FUNNY !

MOSTLY TRUE !

Every diver should read this book!

Every diver should OWN this book!

The Scuba Snobs live in Lakewood, Colorado and have been married almost 30 years. Dennis practices law and teaches part time at an area University. Debbie is a former high school teacher who now works as a legal assistant in and manages Dennis' law practice. They have been diving throughout the Pacific and the Caribbean. They really are nice people. Ok, Debbie is a nice person. Dennis is kind of nice. Sometimes.